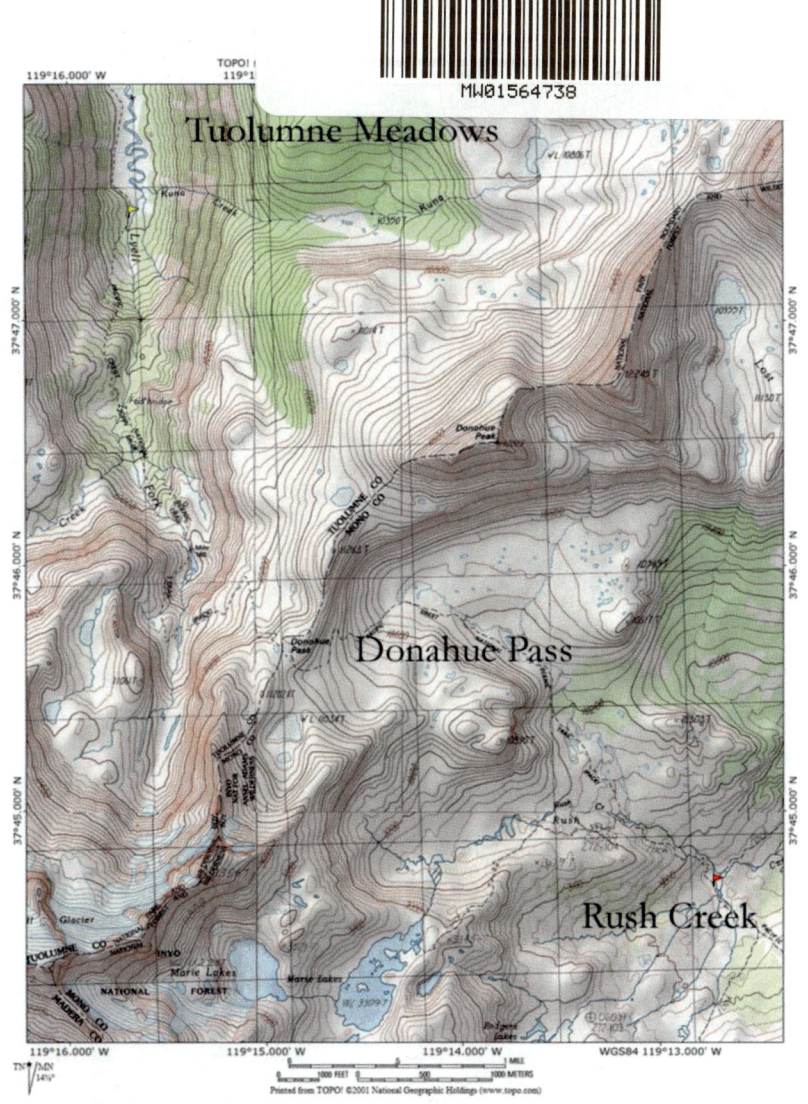

Please join me –

it is always more fun to hike with a friend.

Charles Weeden

Rush Creek

Last night, we camped on Rush Creek (red flag above) on the John Muir Trail just east of Yosemite National Park. Today's hike takes us over Donahue Pass, where we join Lyell Creek and then downstream to Tuolumne Meadows (yellow flag).

We start at an elevation of 9,600 feet, climb to over 11,000 across the pass, and then back down to 9,000. We'll cross from the Rush Creek watershed into the Tuolumne. These cascading, laughing waters that serenaded us last night empty into Mono Lake, a terminal lake with no outlet. These rushing waters need not, for they will sink to the bottom of Mono Lake and grow stagnant. There, they remain for hundreds of years until one day, by chance, they arrive at the surface of the lake and gain escape through evaporation.

Lyell Creek conjoins the Tuolumne River in Tuolumne Meadows and, as one, joyously cascades through the foothills of the Sierra until merging with the San Joaquin River outside of Modesto. Through the sloughs of the Delta, into San Francisco Bay and, on a strong tide, becomes the Pacific.

I am reminded of Bertrand Russel's words:

An individual human existence should be like a river: small at first, narrowly contained within its banks, and rushing passionately past rocks and over waterfalls. Gradually, the river grows wider, the banks recede, and the waters flow more quietly. In the end, without any visible break, they merge in the sea and painlessly lose their individual being.

A metaphor for today, but we get ahead of ourselves.

It is early morning, and the light has not yet hit our campsite, though it reflects the peaks of Banner and Ritter. It is also early autumn, and the John Muir Trail is dry, deserted, and beautiful. The sky is a perfect azure blue.

Such a day is our hope and the why we're here. What fun to have the day and your company ahead.

Climbing out of Rush Creek

My pack is heavy. I lift it each morning, hoping it is lighter as our provisions disappear. But it isn't. I stagger the first few steps and breathe hard after a dozen. Our trail ascends steeply following the water's course. We walk the first half mile in silence, anxious for our bodies to make their aerobic adjustments. After a mile, the trail breaks from the creek, and instead of dirt and rocks, we find ourselves hiking on the white polished granite of the High Sierra. It reflects the angled sun of the early morning and appears as ice.

    We rest a moment and look back towards Rush Creek and its path into Mono. I breathe deeply with my arms akimbo. My body is still fighting to find its second wind. The azure sky is lighter, and a couple of wisps of crest clouds appear atop Ritter, formed by the upward deflection of moist air from the Pacific.

    With my wind somewhat recovered, I offer the day's first words. "So, friend, miles of switch-backs lay ahead. How shall we pass the time?"

    "All journeys begin with a single step; life with a cry and effect with cause."

    "Shall we tell stories, Canterbury-like?"

    "I have no breath to talk – a sedentary life has taken its toll. However, please tell as many tales as pleases you. I'm here to hear."

    "You suggest I walk to talk? We need a topic requiring little talk and much thought. Long contemplative pauses with only occasional gems of perspicacity. Mine the mind, if you will – to keep our minds off the grind."

"If you want to be like that, let's speak of weighty things to keep our minds off weighty packs."

"Well, if it is weightiness you wish – at least mentally – we must speak rarefied thoughts in this rarefied air."

"Yes, perfect, for if our bodies must be punished, so shall our minds."

"But it is all in the mind."

"My lungs, feet, and legs most heartily disagree. A theory I indubitably doubt."

"As is doubt. *Cognito ergo sum*. Wasn't it Descartes who started the migraine of European philosophy?"

"Yes, *Cognito* started it, and, in passing, let me say that I'm beginning to doubt more than just Rene."

"Ah, Rene, you renegade. You started an argument that has gone from the truth that must be found within the mind to the truth that must come from one's perception of the world – philosophical switchbacks without progress. Rationalism to empiricism; empiricism to rationalism. We've made more progress in the last hour than philosophy did in 400 years."

"So, great trailblazing scout, how do you presume to get us off our rutted path?"

"We do so by taking the discussion up a notch. Descartes started with something he felt could not be denied: A construct which all will agree, a foundation for an edifice of truth. But his flaw is that his 'thought' is different than my 'thought.' 'I think' starts at too low a level. It is saying that my migraine feels the same as yours. But how would one ever know?"

"Or my painful side stitch is the same as yours – to use a more apt analogy."

"We must take our starting point up several levels and commence at our highest commonplace. For instance, take speech. I know my brain is not wired exactly like yours, but we have both learned to speak and at this level, we communicate. If we had to compare neuronal wiring and synaptic firings each time we spoke, we'd trip on our first words."

"Or rock. Up a notch. God speed. Anything elevating me today is most welcome."

"So let's start at the highest level we can find and work down until we agree on a common concept. Let's not start with 'I think,' let's start with 'we concur.'"

"So, you're saying we should've started this morning at the pass rather than Rush Creek? I couldn't agree more."

"Let's call our highest commonplace, as we do in math, the greatest common divisor or GCD."

"No, please, anything but math — my threshold for pain can't take it. Even Cheney would consider this torture."

"Worse, tortured reasoning. So, our GCD is the equivalent of the highest level of agreement before we can commence any discussion. For instance, if we take the numbers 66 and 99, the greatest common divisor is 33. Of course, each number is divisible by 3, but we'll save a great deal of time if we skip 3 and start our discussion with 33. That makes sense, right? What's the GCD upon which we both agree."

"Rush Creek definitely was a 3."

"But this is hard because it has to be something we will build on today. So, of the many theories and ideologies that abound, is there one that you feel, intellectually and in the gut, is correct? Or let's put it another way, which concept, if found false, would most surprise you?"

"Hmm, good question. It may take me quite a long time to ponder—at least the next 10 switchbacks. Einstein could be wrong, but since I've never understood his theories, I'm not sure I'd know the difference. Quantum physics could be wrong and doesn't feel right in my gut. Religious doctrines? Since I don't believe in a heaven, karma, reincarnation, or voodoo, they can't be candidates. I have to say that of all I can think of right now, in my anerobic state, I would be most surprised if we didn't evolve but rather were created by another being or entity. For me, evolution and natural selection make sense. There is evidence it is intuitive and feels right. Yep, that is my choice. What's yours?"

"Extraordinary – we already agree. We've got our GCD. If only this trail were so easy. Unlike most theories, everyone can understand the basics of natural selection. As Darwin admits, his theory breaks down if only one living feature could be found not to have arisen through natural selection. Everyone has been trying to find such an exception for 150 years and can't. Even with Newtonian physics, we knew there was a problem with the orbit of Mercury. If that 'problem' were found with evolution, then the theory is disproved, and the Creationists miraculously delivered."

"And, the more research is done, the more convincing the theory of natural selection becomes."

"Okay, so we do have a base that we both believe. And I submit we've progressed farther than Descartes ever got: Two minds in agreement."

"So, what do you propose we do with this flash of insight? Aren't we just two people who agree that the sky is blue? I'm not sure I see any great strides there, or here."

"Okay, I'll formally frame it and see if we agree. We are comprised of a genotype or genes that translate themselves into our physical expression or phenotype. Our phenotype is what is actually tested or interpreted by our environment."

"I'm okay with that. So, it's *selectio ergo sum*. Even if I disagreed with you, it sounds like you want to take this somewhere. Speak to your heart's content – I'm in a listening frame of mind."

"But we need some more building. Name another thing you would be shocked to find wasn't true."

"Wait a second, I thought you were going to be doing the talking. Well, give me another switchback or two. Okay, though I'm not sure it really is another 'thing,' more an addendum to the first – there is no heaven or afterlife. This world is not about another. We are here, alive and right now. No nirvana, no waiting virgins. This is all there is."

"It does go with *selectio*, but I agree it is an important aspect of selection. But what changes if everything is looked upon as our mind and body being tested? How much more real does life become? And, really, aren't we here hiking outdoors because we want to re-test ourselves in a natural environment?"

"Of course, I want to see how close I can come to a cardiac."

"You mean, infer an infarction? But testing ourselves changes everything. Here we are focused on taking our next step, a thought that never occurs to us in our everyday lives. We may want a drink of water, again, something that doesn't usually cross our minds. We want our packs to disappear and to ease into our favorite chairs. But we crave this test – a getting back to our basics. But living with death does more: It focuses our lives and forces us to realize that we can only do a small percentage of those things we want to do."

"Yep, no doubt about the water and the chair. Or a beer! That would be heaven! My kingdom for a beer!"

"Whether it is selection or lack of time, death demands us to make conscious decisions. Where I live precludes me from living in other places I might consider. Coming on this hike prevents me from doing other things."

"What a wonderful idea –other things I could be doing."

"Focus on the now is the only way to be consistent with our two agreed-upon thoughts. Call it selection or Dasein, but we must take Darwin and Heidegger to heart."

"I'm not sure I want to focus on the now right now. How about I just keep thinking about a beer sitting at the end of each switchback – future fantasies to keep my plodding course? Like a paycheck at work."

"Mountain climbers cherish the high they get from challenging death, but what if we create the same thrill every day by denying death through making decisions that, in a sense, defy death? Focus on making the one decision you believe you should be doing. Heidegger calls this 'being in time'.

"But I don't like defying death, which is why, boy genius, I don't mountain climb. Good God, do these switchbacks go on forever?"

"We can have a long-term mountain climber high from emotionally and psychologically living in the shadow of death."

"Damn, but don't that high feel good right now."

"For instance, this Mountain Warbler must eat today. If it makes the wrong choice, it may die. However, for whatever reason, it chooses to come here and discovers

Manzanita berries. It had other options, but it made a decision because it knew that postponing feeding was not an option. How many other choices did it have? Did it make the 'best' choice? The prospect of hunger and thirst brought it purpose and focus. And though it sounds weird, I submit meaning."

"Nothing sounds weird at this point, but I'm not sure the Warbler feels your 'high' just because he found some berries. But aren't you confusing selection with more elevated human decision-making? I may focus on survival in my present state, but my thoughts typically engage at a higher level."

"I don't think so. But first, we must make another rule: If you can't find an exception, you must stay with the rule. The same argument we have with Darwinian evolution. In other words, unless and until you can show me that an activity violates selection, we must continue to think of human activity as selection. Let's say, for instance, that a critical aspect of natural selection is food. So, as living creatures, we have to decide how to find food. Most of us go to work to have those means, but this makes your job, your commute, and your boss all elements in finding food. Until you prove the exception, selection applies."

"You mean this Warbler commuted up Rush Creek to his job in the Manzanita factory?"

"What's the difference? Heck, all aspects of culture can be subsumed into the environment testing of and interpreting our phenotype. How does playing your guitar to your girlfriend any different than this Warbler singing to find his mate?"

"I'm working on the rebuttal. No questions for the witness at this time."

"We all admit that it is 'hard to believe' that the eye or brain is a product of evolution or that our jobs are no different than our Warbler's search for food. To separate them requires an instance of hard evidence. Just like asking our witness, 'If you have an alibi, if you can tell me where you were when the crime was committed, you'll go free.'"

"Okay, okay, but still, humans use logic and animals, instinct, and there is a difference. For instance, we can logically deduce that Manzanita bushes are on the mountain; it is the time of year for berries, and berries are nutritious. We use our logic for survival, not animal instinct. Logic and thought differentiate us. It is a very different process."

"But you're trying to ascribe different internal processes to the external activity that both of you sing or eat berries. That's a violation of our GCD rule. If the thought or the activity is the same, we reset and don't delve below that level. Your contention that instinct and logic are different is irrelevant, for there is no discernible difference between the

Warbler and ourselves eating the berries. Although, there is a big difference between the quality of the songs."

"I'll interpret that as a pathetic effort at a compliment."

"We have to use our philosophical razor – if two activities are the same, we assume the same intention. Though it is difficult for us to believe that our logic and the Warbler's instincts are the same, until there is proof, we must."

"Ah, that's bullshit sophistry."

"I should ask, 'How do you know?' and ceaseless effort at trying to find the final substrate is what sent philosophy into a deduction Charybdis for so long. Let's take a different approach – what is called pragmatism, an American tradition of philosophy from Peirce to James, who asked, 'How is that difference – instinct or logic – useful? Does calling it one or the other make a difference? The berries are still being eaten. What is the 'cash value' as James used to say of your distinction?"

"I'm not sure how it is useful to make both my body and head hurt, but I'm working on a rebuttal."

"But just as our neural wiring may be different, we both can speak; we speak, and the Warbler sings, which is, I contend, different without a difference."

"I wonder if you can actually make my head hurt more than my body. Why don't you give it a shot?"

"How are these daily decisions made – eating berries, getting a job, or taking someone out to dinner? I think it helps to discuss interpretation or, to use a more technical term, hermeneutics. Hermeneutics basically says you have three variables in any interpretation. First, that which the author intends to say or his or her meaning; second, how the intention is communicated or, if you will, the text; and, third, the reader's or viewer's interpretation of the text because there is no way that a reader can directly ascertain the author's intent. Now, much has been written on this, but I think you'll concede that interpreting a book, song, or art involves a combination of meaning, text, and interpretation."

"Hermeneutics has now achieved the improbable – my head hurts more than my legs. Well done!"

"Let's take a Shakespearian play. Shakespeare clearly has intent and meaning; he communicates these in the play's text, and you, as the reader, form your own subjective opinion as to what the text means. Your interpretation may or may not align with Shakespeare's. Each component in an interpretation, Shakespeare's intent, the play itself, and the reader's interpretation aren't all equal aspects in the final interpretation, but I think we can agree that all three are components, right?"

"Sure, that's pretty obvious. But wait, this gives me an argument separating instinct from logic. This is the hard evidence that forces us, rather you, to concede the exception. Animals can't understand Shakespeare. The razor goes dull – challenge that my friend!"

"Wait, what do you mean, understand? Do you mean understanding Shakespeare's intention, understanding his words, or interpreting them as a reader – either animal or human?"

"Don't pull that bullshit – understand it from the reader's interpretation."

"So if I give an English version of King Lear to someone who can't read English, and if they were to page dutifully through the play, allowing a respectful and appropriate time between each page turn, then what do we have?"

"That's a ridiculous. Of course, you have to have someone who reads English."

"Do animals read English?"

"Of course not."

"What is the difference between our non-English reader and a chimp who also dutifully pages through the play?"

"Give me a break. If we provided a translation in the reader's language, then our reader would understand, but the chimp still cannot."

"But what if the reader can't read? What then?"

"More bullshit – the BS meter is flashing in the red zone."

"But you're saying that the understanding depends not on the reader but on the actual text of the play, correct?"

"Yes, that's right."

"So, if we handed the chimp a chimp translation, it would understand."

"But there is no chimp translation as there is no chimp language."

"I suspect you're wrong, but if the substance of Shakespeare could be communicated to a chimp, they would interpret it correctly."

"No, how could they understand the human dimension of Shakespeare?"

"So now we are concerned with the intention of Shakespeare, not the reader's interpretation nor the text, is that right?"

"I think so."

"But female chimps are forced out of their natal family groups so as to not interbreed with the males, so I think at some level they very well understand the issue of being forced out of a family. In fact, they might understand King Lear far better than you do."

"This discussion is as maddening as these bloody switchbacks."

"Well, even if you don't agree, based on our philosophical razor, if we can't agree that something is different, we must treat them as the same. Until you convince me, we must treat decisions and interpretation as the same. We have plenty of time and can switch to baseball and the World Series if you like. But let me at least finish the thought on our three aspects of interpretation."

"Be my guest – you're doing the talking, and it is, at least, a distraction."

"Let's keep testing our model to see if we can find one that doesn't work. If not, then our model must be embraced. Let's discuss your girlfriend – that should take your minds off the trail – and map our interpretative model to your actions. First, you have your intention, which I think best if we leave alone; second, the actual song and the performance of such; and, of course, the intended interpretation of the performance. Obviously, your goal is to convey your meaning into an interpretation effectively. But, quite possibly, she looks at you but only thinks of something or someone else."

"Bad example, for my singing compels complete submission. But let me try one. Your intent in all this is to hike in this absolutely spectacular place, but to kill time, you play mind-numbing games. The text is your circuitous dialogue with this insistence that everything has to be treated as one. And the interpreter can interpret this to whatever meaning I make of it all. My interpretation doesn't have to align with your intent, correct? So here's the verdict – utter crap."

"Correct. But by making that statement, you clearly show that your interpretation is aligned with my intent."

"Never let up, do you? But I think I've found a problem. What if we are trying to interpret something with no meaning?"

"Surely, you don't mean this dialogue."

"I should, but no. How about interpreting this hike over Donahue Pass? It is inanimate and has no meaning as such – it IS. Mangling, I suggest your model. The author has no intention; the text is the mountain, and the interpretation is frustration and remorse."

"Ah, come on. Aren't we having fun yet?"

"But the interpretation of the hike becomes exclusively the interpretation of the authors – us. Worse, it becomes totally subjective. Wipes out your three-part model."

"Now you're sounding like Derrida, but what if I was painting and wiping my brush on a white cloth. You come by, look at the cloth, and admire it as a work of art. I'm not sure it is any different. Is there meaning or intent? No, but there is text and interpretation. If we were to quantify each aspect of this process, it might be M(eaning) – 0%, T(ext) – 20%, and I(interpretation) – 80% of the overall interpretation."

"So, you had to go quantitative? The blessed recourse of all Western thought."

"It is interesting to think through which component constitutes an interpretation. With the art cloth, you, as the reader, can interpret it as you wish: A cloth for wiping my paintbrush or a work of art. The text imposes an interpretation upon the reader; however, the reader is free to choose."

"Interpret this." (A gesture.)

"Nice, but I interpret you're upwards indication as a positive sign that you want to continue our hike towards the pass. Does this interpretation align with your intent?"

"Not close."

"But back to our white cloth, what if I had carefully worked out the splash of paint with long thought intention? Does that make your interpretation more or less valid?"

"Less, I should think."

"I'm not sure. For instance, if the artist of the splash were me, you would continue to think it a mere paint cloth. If, however, I was a famous painter, you would believe it to be art. In this case, the actual text of the art must include the artist's name, which, in turn, changes your interpretation."

"Yep, knowing you, I would never consider it art."

"But why does your interpretation change? Well, if you say something, it will, in turn, be interpreted by someone. You want whoever interprets your comments to interpret that you are knowledgeable in the arts."

"My head hurts. Which I interpret as a lack of oxygen and any proximate commonsense."

"Each interpretation may and must be looked at only in the context of other interpretations. For instance, what if you and a well-known art critic were both looking at my splash painting, and the art critic said that it was a defining piece of art in the 21st Century? Suddenly, your negative opinion of my work turns into a positive comment on my evocative use of color and how the paint swipes look as if someone was cleaning their paintbrush."

"I would never say such a thing."

"Or take that comment. If said as a declarative, I would interpret it one way, but as you said, it with a tone that is part of the text. From your tone, I know you're sarcastic. This might be represented as M-25%, T-50%, I-25%."

"Or, M-0%, T-0% and I-150%."

"Even more sarcasm – switchbacks of sarcasm. Not from your tone but from my interpretation. This brings the score to M-25%, T-25%, and I-50%."

"My 'I' is sinking to 0%."

"Then, time for a break. Let's rest here at this shoulder of Donahue."

Shoulder

We take out our water and gorp. We can clearly see the pass, but miles of scree, erratics, and glaciated granite are ahead.

I rest on the edge of a rock and lean back so that the rock lifts my pack from my shoulders. I take only a tiny sip of water and leave it in my mouth. My body waits for a swallow, but I know it won't assuage my thirst, and I linger on the luxury of its wetness."

"Didn't know warm, polypropylened water could taste this good."

Only some of the switchbacks below are visible but still show our serrated progress from Rush Creek.

"11:00 – four hours – 1,500 feet and who knows how many switchbacks. How are you feeling? The end is in sight."

"How about lunch and a nap?"

"Alongside Lyell Creek."

"I was afraid you'd say that."

We start again. It is hard to return to the slow, plodding rhythm of before. I place a small pebble in my mouth to stimulate saliva. I purposely go slow enough to breathe through my nose and fall several paces behind. I let our earlier thoughts percolate through my consciousness.

"So even I concede all your bullshit, what do we have? Some Darwinian stuff and some interpretive stuff. Two divergent concepts – rationalism and empiricism – not really any different than what we had before. You keep talking about forcing everything into a single model, yet here we are, just like the song: *'Torn between two lovers, feeling like a fool. Loving both of you is breaking all the rules.'* I thought you might like to hear my Warbler-like song. But, from my perspective, you've been hoisted by your own petard."

"Okay, you're a figurative and iterative 'step ahead.' But look at these switchbacks; it may feel like all we're doing is going back and forth; one way, then back the other like thesis, antithesis, but no synthesis. We need to raise the conversation up to a synthesis or what Gadamer calls our 'Ur' or a higher-level direction."

"Our 'ur'? Are you serious? Sounds like you're choking. So, we need an Ur direction. Okay, what is it, Dr. Urologist?"

I laugh, actually now choking on my pebble.

"You okay?"

"Yes." I spit out the pebble.

"Could be you're a philosopher-astronomer who looks upwards at Uranus. Ur anus, get it?"

"I get it."

"And be sure to warn me tonight if you're a uranist."

"Enough, already."

"Okay, I'll stop. Here?"

"Back to your petard point. You're right. We can't call it progress unless we meld evolution and interpretation into an Ur synthesis."

(Continuing.) "*Torn between two theories feeling like a fool....* How does the rest go? Oh, '*There's been another theory that I've needed and I've loved, but that doesn't mean I love you less,*'"

"Here, suck on this pebble."

"*The theory knows it can't possess me, and it knows it never will, there's just this empty place inside of me that only sense can fill.*"

"Wait a second; the genes can produce the text or, let's say, the phenotype. What is selection but the interpretation of one's text? Damn, this is cool. In 20th-century hermeneutics, we have Meaning, Text, and Interpretation; in Darwinian selection, we have genotype, phenotype, and environmental selection. These really are just the same, though, one from the humanities and one from the sciences. What do you think?"

"I think I'll go back to my singing."

"But let's see if it works. We'll try the acid test – will it help us analyze me, rather, my meaning?"

"*Shorn between two theories...*"

"Let's start, 'What's my Text?' And, what interpretation results? Since we can only use the tools we have so far, we don't need to flounder in the metaphysics of the meaning of life, why am I here, or is there a telos beyond living?"

"Right, absolutely no metaphysics, or I call a medivac."

"If I am not living for anything to render meaning, no afterlife or reincarnation, am I living to live? Yes, I think that's correct. Living becomes my meaning. It is an affirmative statement and gives an Ur direction though not telos."

"I have telos – a beer."

"A 'living meaning' declares something. I am not unique as I share 99.99+% of my genes with other humans, but that doesn't deny me an individuality based on my interpretation. I create my own meaning."

"I mean, meaning is really what I mean to mean. Is that what you mean?"

"Yep, never said better. But there is method and madness here. What then constitutes what I am is not meaning but my interpretation. If you will, not the subject but the object in life's sentence. And as each interpreter makes his or her own interpretation, we are unique whether we intend it from our interpretation or not. Are you following?"

"I'm in front, but behind."

"This is great stuff. So, if my interpretation changes, how do I exist? Am I not a body of water? My shape remains, though that which constitutes me, flows through me. My interpretations change me as cascading, laughing waters. As such, I cannot grow stagnant."

"And I am more like these rocks – caring only for immobility."

"And to get downright giddy from either hypoxia, exhaustion, or excitement, if I exist as an interpretation, then my designations – name, occupation, residence – are meaningless."

"Remind me that I need to wash my car the next time you ask me on one of these hikes. Though this is all well and good, it begs another 'Ur' question. What if something cannot be presented in 'text.' Something incommunicable? Then, we have no basis for interpretation except M-0%, T-0%, and I-100%. What happens then to the model? Though we were able to deal with the M as 0%, I don't see how you can have the T be 0%. You're dead-ended, stymied, cul-de-sac'd."

"Hmm. Interesting."

"You end up with a world of pure relativism. Just what happens if someone claims a transcendental vision? I think this might be the exception unless you plan to pull another Ur out of your pocket."

"For if I interpret a transcendental, it must exist, and the Interpretation subsequently becomes the Meaning. Thus, M-0%, T-0%, I-100% really is M-0%, T-0%, I-100%, M-100%, T-x%, I-x% and so on. This is beautiful – each interpretation becomes the next meaning, and cascades ever gather more interpretations until one senses they are all one."

"Like a trail?"

"A watershed – a concatenation of interpretations that acts as an ecosystem or a neural network. A living, interacting network in which each interpretation reverberates within the web, affecting all of our meanings. And 'hitches' as Muir said while hiking on this eponymous trail, to everything else in the Universe."

Donahue Pass

We plod our last few uphill steps through jagged scree. The western wind hits us in the face. For the past hour, we have been looking at little more than the few feet ahead of our feet, and now we confront a view that stretches to the Pacific. Our bodies are exhausted with energy.

We sit, eat our gorp, try to trace the lines of the rivers, and, too soon, put our arms back into our harnesses and enjoy the first downhill steps of the day.

We pass the tarn at the foot of the Donahue glacier and walk through the rivulets that form from the seepage from the small meadow. The drop is extremely steep, and our path is the Lyell Creek stream bed. There is no room between the rock outcroppings for both.

We follow the creek for the next 8 miles and leave it at Tuolumne Meadows. We watch as the water, which both is and of the river, continues its course to the Pacific.

Transcendence and a beer, not evaporation, become us.

Made in United States
Orlando, FL
14 May 2024